ENGLISH

LESSONS
AT A MOMENT'S NOTICE

ENGLISH

LESSONS AT A MOMENT'S NOTICE

by Barbara Murray

W. FOULSHAM & CO. LIMITED

LONDON · NEW YORK · TORONTO · CAPE TOWN · SYDNEY

W. FOULSHAM & CO. LIMITED
Yeovil Road, Slough, Berks., England

ISBN 0-572-01362-0

© W. Foulsham & Co. Limited, 1986

Typeset by C. R. Barber & Partners (Highlands) Ltd.,
Fort William, Scotland
Reproduced, printed and bound in Great Britain by
Hazel Watson & Viney Limited,
Member of the BPCC Group,
Aylesbury, Bucks

Acknowledgements

The author and publisher are grateful for
permission to reproduce the following:

DULCE ET DECORUM EST
The estate of Wilfred Owen and Publishers
Chatto & Windus: The Hogarth Press.

A DISSERTATION UPON ROAST
PIG by Charles Lamb from *Essays of Elia*
(Everyman's Library) published by J. M.
Dent.

BRER RABBIT, THE ELEPHANT
AND THE WHALE from *101 School
Assembly Stories* by Frank Carr, published by
W. Foulsham & Co. Ltd.

Contents

Contents

Introduction

This book is about English in all its forms: the written and the spoken; poetry and prose; sentences, phrases and words.

But it is not a text book. It is intended for teachers who will have to take over at a moment's notice without the luxury of time to prepare materials and choose extracts for study. Accordingly, each unit has been designed so that the only aids required are a board and chalk (or their equivalents) for the teacher, and pencils and paper for the students.

The units themselves are a series of suggestions for 'one off' lessons which may or may not have any follow-up; thus mountains of marking for the relieving and the returning teacher are avoided. Above all, it is hoped that the lessons will be seen as imaginative, positive and often entertaining. (There is no logical reason why learning should ever be dull.) This will help to alleviate the problems that accompany the teaching of an unfamiliar class by an unfamiliar teacher in an unaccustomed role. The teacher's function here is seen as that of a guide to the discovery of new ways through old mazes.

The units are designed to be practical in nature so that pupils will 'learn through doing' and thus be helped on their way to a fuller understanding of the workings and power of words.

To develop a mastery of the language, the pupil must develop a way of looking at things accurately, of experiencing things fully, and of expressing things clearly.

It is hoped that the creative acts demanded of the pupils will enable them to do this; thus they will learn to make decisions, select ideas, and bring critical capacities into play.

All the units are directly or indirectly based on exercises and activities which pupils have been found to enjoy. The author knows them to be workable and effective for pupils through a range of ages and abilities, giving an outlet for self-expression which sometimes, seemingly, has no direct relevance to native intelligence.

To facilitate the choosing of material, all units have level indicators denoting relative complexity of the material to be used. *Level A* is intended to be a simpler exercise; *Level B* a more complex one; while *Level C* is for more able or advanced pupils. It is important to remember, however, that *grading is a relative exercise*. The final choice of level and material must be left to the judgement of the teacher. The ideas presented could be adapted further to suit a particular class or need; in that case they will form the basis for other imaginative work and presentations.

The units themselves are divided thematically into 4 sections, each based on one particular skill, followed by some classroom quizzes.

1 FUN WITH WORDS deals with *vocabulary building* and word power

2 SOLVE THIS ONE comprises *problem-solving* units

3 TALK IT OUT involves *guided discussion*

4 EVERYONE'S A WRITER aims to build confidence in *writing creatively*, both in poetry and prose.

The units are worded for the teacher, giving a *suggested level* and *class organisation* (both of which will depend on the class make-up and on the strengths and style of the individual teacher), an *introductory comment* to establish the content of the unit, and *instructions on the running* of the unit. Materials to be written on the board are listed clearly and answers are given to all exercises.

Because of the nature of the book, the units are not intended to be linked sequentially in any way. They are simply a series of individual lessons, grouped under thematic headings, which will cover a 40 minute period. Thus they can be dipped into at random. Where feedback sessions are indicated, these can be as long or short as the teacher finds necessary. Some units suggest possibilities for further work or follow up at home.

At the end of the book there is a work sheet on which can be recorded those units that have been used by the different classes. This could be helpful to Supply teachers who may not know the 'history' of the classes they are meeting.

Fun with Words

Vocabulary study

1 CRISSCROSS (Levels A, B & C)

1   Divide the class into groups of 3 or 4.

2   Ask the pupils to give you *any* 5 words they can think of off the tops of their heads. You might get one word from each group. (These words should not seem to be related.)

   e.g.   POLICEMAN SUNSHINE ANXIETY
          SENSITIVE MOUNTAIN

3   Write the words on the board in the following pattern, as they are fired at you:

POLICEMAN   SENSITIVE

                          ANXIETY

SUNSHINE   MOUNTAIN

4   Giving the groups *10 minutes maximum*, ask the pupils to make word associations diagonally. They should start in the corners and work towards the centre till it is seen that each of the corner words is linked with the centre word.

A finished example might look like this:

POLICEMAN   SENSITIVE

patrol   appearance

robbers   jokes

guns

ANXIETY

cancer   climbers

sunburn   avalanche

snowstorm

SUNSHINE   MOUNTAIN

5   After the time is up, have the groups compare their creations. These could be read out, written on the board by you, or, with a small number of groups, one 'scribe' for each group could write the contributions on the board.

6   Begin subsequent rounds with further sets of 5 words from the groups.

If you know beforehand that the pupils you are to take have been studying specific words in class or for homework, you could give a selection of 5 words from these lists to start the game off.
An element of competition can be built into the game by seeing which group can create the longest list of associations before reaching the word in the centre.

2 CRAZYGRAMS (Levels A, B & C)

1   Divide the class into small groups of not more than 4 pupils.

2   Ask each group in turn to give you a letter of the alphabet.

Write these letters on the board in a horizontal line. (You might start with a selection of 6 or 7 letters.)

e.g.   M C B F P W E
         I W H J D T C A X

3   Give the groups 3 or 4 minutes to make imaginative and correctly constructed sentences out of the letters. Each letter should begin a word. The words should be kept in the order of the letters originally supplied.

e.g.   Many Children Buy Funny Postcards Without Envelopes
         I Wonder How John Decided To Choose An X

4   At the end of the set time have a spokesman for each group read out the result of the combined effort. A vote can be taken for the most original contribution, and points can be given to the winning team. (See Note 1 at end.)

For pupils at Level A, connectors such as AND, and BUT, and prepositions such as OF and FROM can be used. Pupils can also make use of the 'telegramese' 'STOP' to make more than one sentence.

The game can be made more difficult for the B & C levels by:

a   increasing the number of letters;

b   forbidding the use of connectors and prepositions between the words;

c   penalising groups for the use of 'STOP' to create new sentences. (One point can be deducted for each instance of the word.)

Note 1   Alternatively, have an official Panel of Judges. Each group chooses a judge. The panel awards 3, 2 or 1 point for each sentence according to its appeal.
          Judges cannot vote for their own groups.

Note 2   With more mature students, the panel can be elected officially (each one nominated, seconded and voted for) so that one can restrict the panel to a small (but odd) number, say 5 or 3.

The panel can then help make the rules, in addition to judging.
Again, a judge may not vote (on the 3, 2, 1 system) for the group he came from.

The reading aloud of the contributions can be as educative as the creation of them – and possibly very entertaining.

3 MAGIGRAPHS (Levels A, B & C)

This exercise encourages freedom of structure in writing by experimentation with form. Pupils can work individually, or in pairs.

The idea is to choose a subject that can be conveyed in an optical and original design, but using words and phrases to create the shapes required.

The content of the writing should be sensible, and appropriate to the shape being created.

To provide inspiration, you could create a 'magigraph' on the board with the help of the class.

Take, for example, the idea of *AN UMBRELLA*.

Ask the class for simple words or phrases that they think describe an umbrella well. Write the words in a list on the board. Your list might look like this:

rainbow colours	joyful
silk	wet slopes
protection	glisten
shelter	bobbing
happy	

Now, using these words as your tools, create the shape of an umbrella. (You may want the pupils to help you fit the words together.)

rainbow colours,   silken slopes

protecting, joyfully bobbing, glistening

our shelter in a storm

Another example takes the idea of *THE DEAD TREE*.

wind shrieks through naked arms

of the life that was

the lonely sentinel stands a skeleton

the last of the old guard gnarled fingers twist skywards

Note Here we are using clauses and sentences rather than phrases.

Have the pupils choose their own subjects and write their own 'magigraphs'.

Some suggestions for subjects could be:

The Mouse

Man

The Sun

A Bus

A Spring Flower

A Cloud

A Happy Home

An Unhappy Home

With more advanced students, or the more sensitive and perceptive, it might be worthwhile to try one or two abstract ideas, e.g. Happiness, Growing Up, or even God.

It will be interesting to see what 'shape' is given to these ideas by the more imaginative young people.

4   ANAGRAMS   (Levels A, B & C)

This is a good activity to test both spelling and knowledge of the subject areas chosen for the groups of anagrams.

The activity may be done in groups with a time limit imposed by you to provide a competitive element to the exercise.

If a more leisurely approach is required, the activity may be done by individual pupils working at their own pace.

For Levels A & B, to aid pupils in their search for the correct words, the first letters of the unscrambled words could be given, e.g. B A Y I L → L

The following sets could be used at the suggested levels:

1 COUNTRIES OF THE WORLD (Geography/General Knowledge)

LEVEL A

AUSRIS	RUSSIA
TRIBNIA	BRITAIN
AMYGREN	GERMANY
CARFEN	FRANCE
TUKYER	TURKEY
ANDACA	CANADA
WEN LAZNEAD	NEW ZEALAND
LATASAURI	AUSTRALIA
NAHIC	CHINA
DIALNATH	THAILAND
NAIDI	INDIA

LEVEL B

CORCOOM	MOROCCO
TRAASUI	AUSTRIA
MOASA	SAMOA
AMNO	OMAN
RESAIL	ISRAEL
VAGYLOUSIA	YUGOSLAVIA
GEARAIL	ALGERIA
GROUPLAT	PORTUGAL
PEGTY	EGYPT
READOUC	ECUADOR
MAPNAA	PANAMA

LEVEL C

BAYIL	LIBYA
OHATIPEI	ETHIOPIA
ZIMQUAMBOE	MOZAMBIQUE
EGUNIA	GUINEA
NYEEM	YEMEN
REBOON	BORNEO
GRABAILU	BULGARIA
SHELTERNAND	NETHERLANDS
LOSTDANC	SCOTLAND
YAGAUN	GUYANA

2 **ANIMALS** (General Knowledge)

LEVEL A

WEE	EWE
FARFIGE	GIRAFFE
TALEPHEN	ELEPHANT
BALLWAY	WALLABY
MOPHISAUPTOP	HIPPOPOTAMUS
PEELTOAN	ANTELOPE
LARGOIL	GORILLA
TOYCOE	COYOTE
EYHAN	HYENA
FULABOF	BUFFALO

3 **COUNTIES OF BRITAIN** (Geography/Secretarial Studies)

LEVELS B & C

LCRNAWOL	CORNWALL
FULKOFS	SUFFOLK
THORDERF	HERTFORD
REHITSWIL	WILTSHIRE
STILERECE	LEICESTER
NINCOLL	LINCOLN
RYBED	DERBY
FEDDY	DYFED
IRYRSKOHE	YORKSHIRE
BUCIMAR	CUMBRIA

4 RIVERS OF THE WORLD (General Knowledge/Geography)

LEVELS B & C

RAMRUY	MURRAY
HATSEM	THAMES
NOZAAM	AMAZON
DAN GORIRE	RIO GRANDE
PISMIPISSIS	MISSISSIPPI
SURIMOIS	MISSOURI
TENAMOCARS	SACRAMENTO
GAUWNIAN	WANGANUI
LINE	NILE
POMOILP	LIMPOPO

5 **FOODS** (Home Economics)

LEVELS A & B

THEGSPAIT	SPAGHETTI
REFURBBEGE	BEEFBURGER
GASASUE	SAUSAGE
RECLOWFULIA	CAULIFLOWER
GERMUNIE	MERINGUE
LAMBNACENG	BLANCMANGE
FLOFUSE	SOUFFLE
TOURSTEGEC	COURGETTES
TESREDS	DESSERT
LAPINEPEP	PINEAPPLE

6 **COMPUTER TERMS**

LEVEL A

BOYRAKED	KEYBOARD
ORRCUS	CURSOR
SLAVERAIB	VARIABLES
PYSTIME	MISTYPE
REFIVY	VERIFY
MORDAN	RANDOM
SCROOPERS	PROCESSOR
IGCOL	LOGIC
RITOPIRY	PRIORITY
TENGEIR	INTEGER

LEVELS B & C

LOUDROMAT	MODULATOR
RONDCEE	ENCODER
TRISUCIC	CIRCUITS
LIONICS	SILICON
CROLLINGS	SCROLLING
UBOSTUNIER	SUBROUTINE
NEATMURG	ARGUMENT
MORGATILICH	LOGARITHMIC
ZORMINEAD	RANDOMIZE
STABERTUIT	ATTRIBUTES

5 WORD TEASERS (Levels A, B & C)

This activity is best done individually or in pairs. Write the teasers on the board as set out below,

Example

```
    STAND
    ───────
      I
  I UNDERSTAND
```

and get the pupils to work out what they really mean (each could be a word or a phrase).

1 PULL S K C O S	**2** SOCIETY	**3** AN ――――― COAT
4 R O ROADS D S	**5** WE'RE ――――― WORKED	**6** 1 ――――― OTHER
7 WEATHER ――――― HE'S	**8** SI HE'S DE	**9** LIVING ――――― SHOESTRING
10 SDRAW	**11** ――――― RU_N	**12** S R I A T S
13 C LION LION LION	**14** CYCLE CYCLE	**15** TIME / TIME

1	2	3
ME / LOOK	LIVING / CCCC	IIII
4	**5**	**6**
SIDE / SIDE	YOU'RE / BALL	FEET FEET FEET FEET FEET FEET
7	**8**	**9**
OUTSIDE	MAKE ENDSSDNE	MEN MEN MEN MEN
10	**11**	**12**
READING	I'M D E F	INTEREST RATE
13	**14**	**15**
SHE'S / MOON	NRUT	ANT ANT ANT ANT ANT ANT ANT ANT ANT ANT

1 IT ÷ LOOK	**2** M.A. PH.D ——— O	**3** J T RIGHT U S
4 E D I S	**5** SO WE'RE UP	**6** TAKER ——— THE
7 OTHER /1	**8** P U	**9** BIDS BIDS BIDS BIDS
10 B lo O ok O ing K	**11** J U U S S T	**12** MAⒸTERIAL
13 R T ☐ O O	**14** I ————— ESTIMATED	**15** OR OR OR OR OR OR OR OR OR OR

ANSWERS

LEVEL A		LEVEL B		LEVEL C	
1	Pull your socks up	1	Look after me	1	Look into it
2	High Society	2	Living overseas	2	Two degrees above zero
3	An overcoat	3	Eyes right!	3	Just about right
4	Crossroads	4	Side by Side	4	Right side up
5	We're overworked	5	You're on the ball	5	We're in the soup
6	One on top of the other	6	Six Feet tall/high	6	The undertaker
7	He's under the weather	7	Left outside	7	One after the other
8	He's inside	8	Make ends meet	8	Backup
9	Living on a shoestring	9	Foremen	9	Forbids
10	Backwards	10	Reading between the lines	10	Looking through the book
11	Run over	11	I'm fed up	11	Just between us
12	Upstairs	12	Low interest rate	12	See-through material
13	Sealions	13	She's over the moon	13	Square root
14	Bicycle	14	Turn back	14	I overestimated you
15	Time and time again	15	Tenants	15	Tenors

FOLLOW-UP
Now have the pupils create their own teasers.

6 HOMOPHONES (Levels A, B & C)

The following exercise may be done individually, in pairs or in small groups.

Many words in English sound the same but are spelt differently. The following groups of definitions all involve such confusions.

1 Write the pairs of definitions on the board for the pupils to work on to find the homophones (explain the word).

2 Insist on the correct spelling of the two words involved. A time limit may be set to give the more able students a challenge. You may wish to have groups compete to be the first to finish.

Each correctly chosen and spelt word scores a point.
Dictionaries may be allowed if they are available.

LEVEL A   Group 1

		Answers	
naked	an animal	bare	bear
to strike	a vegetable	beat	beet
a great price	an animal	dear	deer
soft hair	a tree	fur	fir
to run away	an insect	flee	flea
a title	darkness	knight	night
large	part of a fire-place	great	grate
did hear	a group of cows	heard	herd
speed of ships	no	knot	not
rest	a part	peace	piece

LEVEL A   Group 2

		Answers	
a series or collection	of pleasant taste	suite	sweet
way or style	a large estate	manner	manor
a town	to bore a hole	borough	burrow

(admit – not quite homophones)

part of a room	sticking down with wax	ceiling	sealing
made from corn	belonging to a series	cereal	serial
a group which makes decisions	to give advice	council	counsel
a shellfish	part of the body	mussel	muscle
gain	a person who foretells events	profit	prophet
a worker underground	a person under age	miner	minor
rose high	a fighting weapon	soared	sword

LEVEL A   Group 3

		Answers	
what you do with a book	a hollow stalk	read	reed
a circle	to twist	ring	wring
part of the ocean	to observe	sea	see
looks at long and hard	a series of steps	stares	stairs
something told	part of an animal	tale	tail
not strong	seven days	weak	week
couple	kind of fruit	pair	pear
use up foolishly	part of the body	waste	waist
the cost of a journey	just	fare	fair
post	masculine	mail	male

LEVEL B   Group 1

		Answers	
the full number	to praise	complement	compliment
the centre of a nut	commander of a regiment	kernel	colonel
chief	a basic truth	principal	principle
a short oar	bones of the head	scull	skull
a type of sign	a musical instrument	symbol	cymbal
to agree to	the act of going up	assent	ascent
made beer	a bird's offspring	brewed	brood
a cleft in the rock	one who harvests the sea	fissure	fisher
one who puts seed in the ground	one who uses a needle	sower	sewer
a special group in India	to throw	caste	cast

LEVEL B   Group 2

		Answers	
a member of the onion family	to let water in or out	leek	leak
a small thing	power	mite	might
a sound of distress	cut down	moan	mown
a bucket	with not much colour	pail	pale
to stop briefly	soft feet of an animal	pause	paws
to ask for urgently	the victim of a hunt	pray	prey
to fly upwards	painful	soar	sore
did fly	a kind of chimney	flew	flue
the noise a horse makes	no (archaic)	neigh	nay
a sheet of glass	ache	pane	pain

LEVEL B   Group 3

a covering for the head	fast running animal	hair	hare
to cry out	a spherical toy	bawl	ball
the sea shore	a tree	beach	beech
not fine	an area for racing	coarse	course
early morning wetness on grass	what is owing	dew	due
the front	the square of two	fore	four
has got bigger	a sound indicating pain	grown	groan
part of the foot	to cure	heel	heal
a kind of deer	vital part of the body	hart	heart
what is lent	alone	loan	lone

LEVEL C   Group 1

		Answers	
want	to work dough	need	knead
to peel	a fruit	pare	pear
empties out	holes in the skin	pours	pores
to knock	to enclose in paper	rap	wrap
proud	a blood vessel	vain	vein
a valley	a cover for the face	vale	veil
rind or skin	a ring of bells	peel	peal
a churchyard tree	a female sheep	yew	ewe
used to propel a boat	metal in its natural state	oar	ore
part of a circle	a biblical vessel	arc	ark

LEVEL C   Group 2

		Answers	
strong beer	to be unwell	ale	ail
what we breathe	one who inherits	air	heir
a tusked animal	to make a hole	boar	bore
a branch	to bend down	bough	bow
a position	to summon	site	cite
to lose life	to stain	die	dye
a measurement of length	a trick	feet	feat
dirty	a bird	foul	fowl
to cut	a colour	hew	hue
a male person	a sacred song	him	hymn

LEVEL C   Group 3

		Answers	
to pierce	a dress ornament	broach	brooch
makes tea	a pressure mark	brews	bruise
the inner part	a body of soldiers	core	corps
destiny	a feast or fair	fate	fête
to adorn with gold	a society for mutual aid	gild	guild
to think	stables	muse	mews
a fruit	a lead weight at the end of a line	plum	plumb
24 sheets of paper	a band of singers	quire	choir
what is sown	to give up	seed	cede
steps over a fence	manner	stile	style

This activity is best done by individuals or pairs. Each of the following words has more than one meaning. Which meaning is intended depends on the different functions the word has in any sentence. For example, the word may both describe something, and be an action word or verb:

a pérfect day

He perféctéd his grammar.

Such words can be easily distinguished in spoken English because the placing of the stress changes with the function of the word:

a pérfect example

He perféctéd his service at tennis.

In writing, these changes are not so easy to show, except by the context in which the word is used.

Now, see if you can show, by composing sentences, that we change the functions (and the pronunciation) of the following words. (*You will need to write two sentences for each word.*)

LEVEL A	LEVEL B	LEVEL C
Perfect	Contract	Defect
Content	Desert	Affix
Produce	Frequent	Discount
Insult	Escort	Recount
Project	Converse	Compress
Refuse	Subject	Invalid
Permit	Prospect	Second
Object	Convict	Accent
Conduct	Suspect	Digest
Reject	Extract	Exploit
Present	Abstract	Minute
Increase		

The use of dictionaries should be encouraged.

This exercise works best if done in small groups (say 5s)

It has been said that there would be no arguments if only people could first agree on the meanings of the words they use.

1   Explain that vague and woolly definitions only confuse others, so the following golden rules must be applied to any explanations that are made: (Write these rules on the board.)

They must be
1 simple and clear
2 correctly expressed
3 specific to the subject being defined

They must *not* be
1 too general
2 too limited
3 too joky to be useful

2   Now write on the board the following definitions. Have the class criticise them according to the rules above.

a   A clock is an instrument for measuring time.
(too general – excludes a watch, a chronometer and a sundial)

b   Ink is a black liquid used for writing.
(too limited – excludes other colours)

c   A cauliflower is a cabbage with a college education.
(clever, but perhaps too joky, and not clear)

d   A stool is a topless chair.
(??)

3   Write the following words on the board and have the pupils in their groups write definitions for them.

LEVEL A	LEVEL B	LEVEL C
Diary	Piano	Geologist
Mustard	Argument	Politician

Blindness	Prune	Boys
Snake	Genius	Anatomy
Breadknife	Words	Telephone
Wrist	Hang-over	Barber
Bicycle	Vacuum cleaner	Terrorist
Violin	Pulpit	Cricket
Kangaroo	King	Scissors
Piano	Camera	Martyr
Mat	Helicopter	Bikini
Fashion	Coward	Undertaker
Fog	Girls	Religion
Music	Sinner	Maths
Hairdresser	Tourist	Climate

When the work is complete (or 10 minutes or so from the end of the lesson), ask each group to appoint one representative to sit on a panel of judges.

The panel then hears the sentences read out and allocates points, 3, 2 or 1 according the the quality (precision) of the sentence.

A judge may not vote on sentences from his/her group.

9 KNOW YOUR QUANTITIES (Levels A, B & C)

This activity can be done in pairs or in groups.

The use of dictionaries should be encouraged.

For the weaker groups, the first letter of the word required could be given.

1   Divide the class into working groups.
Explain that in the Wundaworld Safari Park, the pupils will see groups of animals, birds, insects and fish.
Write the following list of such creatures on the board and ask the pupils to find the word (collective noun) for A GROUP OF each of them:

e.g.   CATTLE   →   a *herd* of cattle

Allow 5–10 minutes for discussion before checking the results.

sheep (flock)	elephants (herd)	fish (shoal)
bees (swarm/flight)	wolves (pack)	locusts (plague)
lions (pride)	insects (cloud)	chickens (brood)
camels (train)	whales (school)	puppies (litter)
badgers (set)	geese (gaggle)	wild geese in flight (skein)

2   Explain that we sometimes use parts of words from other languages to describe how many things we have:

e.g.   *TRICYCLE*   →   3 wheels

QUADRANGLE   has (?) sides

Write the following list of words on the board and ask the pupils to explain how many things they have for each of the words. Allow 5–10 minutes discussion before checking the results with the class. A number of interesting connotations will emerge during the discussion between teacher and class.

hexagon (6)	quintet (5)	unity (1)	sextet (6)
triangle (3)	heptagon (7)	septet (7)	pentagon (5)
monocle (1)	dioxide (2)	bicycle (2)	
century (100)	quadruplets (4)	tetragon (4)	

3   Explain that general objects and people are also given special words to describe a number of them. Write the following list on

the board and have the pupils find the word that we use for A
NUMBER OF each one.
Allow 10 minutes before checking the results with the class.

drawers (chest)	men's clothes (suit)	bells (peal)
eternal time (eon)	actors (troupe)	eggs (clutch)
grapes (bunch)		tears (flood)
stairs (flight)	pictures (gallery)	beauties (bevy)
tables (nest)	playing cards (pack)	witches (coven)
keys (bunch)	ships (fleet)	thieves (gang)
singers (choir)	scissors (pair)	sailors (crew)
office workers (staff)	angry people (mob)	trees (clump or stand)
people in church (congregation)	mountains (chain/range)	cakes (batch)
arrows (quiver)	furniture (suite)	cutlery (canteen)

If time allows, the pupils could be asked to write some of the
more difficult collective nouns in good sentences.

10   KNOW YOUR ADJECTIVES   (Levels B & C)

This is an activity which could be done individually, but it is
probably more effective if done in pairs or small groups that allow for
quiet discussion.
   The use of dictionaries should be encouraged.

1   Divide the class into working pairs or groups.
   Write the following list of places on the board.
   Explain to the pupils that they should find the *ADJECTIVES*
   which come from, or are associated with, these places.
   Allow 10 minutes for discussion before checking on the results
   with the class.

Aberdeen (Aberdonian)	Norway (Norwegian)	Moscow (Muscovite)
Poland (Polish)	Iraq (Iraqi)	Switzerland (Swiss)
Denmark (Danish)	Belgium (Belgian)	Shropshire (Salopian)
Florence (Florentine)	Venice (Venetian)	Wales (Welsh)
Glasgow (Glaswegian)	Eton (Etonian)	Egypt (Egyptian)
Liverpool (Liverpudlian)	Isle of Man (Manx)	Portugal (Portuguese)
Manchester (Mancunian)	Harrow (Harrovian)	Flanders (Flemish)
Oxford (Oxonian)	Naples (Neopolitan)	Yugoslavia (Yugoslav)
Finland (Finnish)	Cornwall (Cornish)	Netherlands (Dutch)
Rome (Roman)	Athens (Athenian)	Cambridge (Cantabrian)

Note: Insist on the correct spelling!

Are there a few local words that can be introduced? e.g. Liverpudlian – Scouse. Do Mancunians have a less formal description? Why 'Salopian' for a Shropshire lad?

2   Write the following list of words on the board.
Explain to the pupils that they should form *ADJECTIVES* from the words.
Again, insist on the correct spelling of the words.
Allow 10 minutes for discussion before checking on the results with the class.

cook (cookery)	nonsense (nonsensical)
fame (famous)	climate (climatic)
clarity (clear)	remedy (remedial)

anxiety (anxious)

authenticity (authentic)

brevity (brief)

prophet (prophetic)

notoriety (notorious)

spectacle (spectacular)

gas (gaseous)

tactics (tactical)

suicide (suicidal)

omen (ominous)

joke (jocular)

diet (dietary)

chaos (chaotic)

nucleus (nuclear)

The discussion of these adjectives can lead into all sorts of interesting by-ways.

3 Explain to the pupils that it often happens that the *NAMES of gods or people* (alive or dead, real or imaginary) are used to form adjectives. Write the following list on the board and ask the pupils:

(a) to find the adjectives from the names given;

(b) to say what the adjectives mean.

Allow 5–10 minutes for discussion before checking the results.

Mercury (mercurial) Hercules (herculean) Jove (jovial)

Pasteur (pasteurised) Mars (martial) Satan (satanic)

Mesmer (mesmerised) Galvani (galvanised)

Many of the words, e.g. galvanised, will need considerable explanation. In fact, each one has a story – making a good subject for research and writing for homework.

Talk it Out

Discussion

11 PRIORITIES (Levels B & C)

1   Write on the board the following list of school subjects:
Mathematics, Music, English language, English literature, Art,
Biology, Physics, French, Cooking, Psychology.

2   Ask the class to consider the list and then suggest some criteria
by which they might classify the subjects.

     e.g.   USEFUL DIFFICULT INTERESTING
              CREATIVE STIMULATING

3   Now divide the class into groups, each of which selects a leader,
and ask the pupils to rate the subjects in order, 1–10, according
to each of the criteria they have given. The group leader will
need to have his/her list ready on paper.

4   Have the groups report back to the class after a set time, say 10
minutes, and discuss the findings. Try and come to some sort of
agreement.

5   Return the students to their groups and ask them to design the
ideal curriculum for their school. Ask them to consider:

a   at what stages subjects should be introduced;

b   which students should take them; and

c   how often the lessons in those subjects should be timetabled each day or week.

6   Have the groups report back their plans for the school. Try and come to a consensus as to what is considered the ideal curriculum for the school. The group decisions may differ widely, in which case the group leader (prompted by her/his members) should be asked to justify their particular plan. Who, for example, would include psychology, and why?

12   SCHOOL HOLIDAYS   (Levels A, B & C)

It has been suggested that: the summer vacation is too long; pupils get bored; parents get fed up with having children around at home all day; teachers think that the long break results in pupils forgetting a lot of what they have learnt (though the experts in psychology say that the brain needs that long rest in order to absorb what has been learnt).

Divide the class into 4 groups to represent the feelings of each of the following sets of people:

a   pupils who agree that the holiday is too long;

b   pupils who disagree, and think the holiday is not long enough;

c   parents who think that the holiday is too long;

d   teachers who see both sides of the argument.

1   Allow the groups up to 10 minutes to discuss the idea and to prepare to argue, with detailed reasons, for their particular viewpoint as pupils (a) or (b), parents or teachers. Impress on the groups that they are to try and persuade the others in the class to their way of thinking. ... And you don't persuade people by ridiculing their arguments. You need to be tolerant, calm and

cunning. Ask each group to elect a leader to present the views of the members of that group.

2　Bring the groups together, to enable leaders to present their ideas to the whole class, and enjoy a full scale, tolerant discussion. Try to get the pupils to come to some majority decision/compromise.

3　Now have the pupils suggest individually what they would consider to be the ideal school year. They should consider:

a　how long the terms should be;

b　how long and how often the holidays should be;

c　when the holiday period should be taken.

4　In groups again, give the pupils the following situation to discuss: Imagine you are members of your local council. You have a budget of £20 000 to be spent on recreational facilities for pupils during the school holidays.
How would you make the holiday period exciting and worthwhile for children?

Have the groups report back on the decisions made in activity No. 4 during the last part of the lesson.

13　**BALLOON DEBATES**　(Levels A, B & C)

Up to 10 famous people are crowded into the basket suspended beneath a hot-air balloon which has a slow leak. The only way to have one survivor of the fated journey is for the others to be thrown out to keep the balloon airborne. The debate has to decide which person in the basket is most worth preserving for the future of mankind.

Preparation for the debate can be done individually, in pairs, or in small groups.

1　Have each person/group choose one famous person, real or fictional, dead or alive.

Get the pupils to work out and note down all the possible
arguments in favour of their choices, including defences against
points that might be brought up by the opposition.

Work should also be done on how best to present the argument
(for example, saving the most important or dramatic point till
last) and on deciding which part of the 'case' each pupil will put
across. (There is no problem here if the task is done individually.
If pairs or groups are used, those not chosen to 'be' the
candidate should assume the roles of seconders and present one
or two extra arguments supporting the claims of their
candidates.)

Allow about 10–15 minutes for this preparation.

2   Have the groups come together for the debate in a semi-formal
    arrangement. Each speaker/group of speakers should present the
    case for the chosen candidate to the class as a whole. Voting
    should be as 'genuine' as possible, and the announcement of the
    survivor by you, the Chairman, ends the activity.

ALTERNATIVE TOPICS FOR THE DEBATES

1   The best form of transport for the general public is:
    car, bicycle, bus, train, roller-skates, horse.

2   The most useful subject to study at school is:
    English, Physics, Cooking, Art, Maths, Music.

3   The best spare-time activity is:
    football, swimming, cooking, computers, train-spotting, reading.

14 ELECTION TIME   (Levels A, B & C)

This is a group activity.

The leader of any country has a difficult job, whether the person is
Prime Minister, President, Dictator, King or Queen.

1   Discuss with the pupils the difference between the different titles

and offices mentioned above. Try and keep the pupils to the facts, not opinions or prejudices (explain the difference).

2　Divide the class into small groups.
Ask each group to list in order of priority the top 10 attributes that they think a good Prime Minister should have, e.g. honesty, toughness, charm, knowledge, experience, determination, good health.
(Allow about 5 minutes for this.)
Now choose one person from each group in turn to write the group's priorities on the board.

3　When all the lists are on the board, have the pupils discuss the ideas presented, and try to come to some majority decision as to which attributes should be possessed.

4　Now choose a candidate for the office of Prime Minister from each group.
Have the group work out together an election speech which will leave the others in no doubt as to who the best candidate is.

5　Run the election campaign.
Have the candidates present their prepared speeches to the whole class with everything they have got!
Votes could be taken, keeping in mind:

a　the quality of the delivery;

b　the ideas presented;

c　the candidate who swept the voters off their feet! i.e. the power of persuasion;

d　the likelihood or possibility of his/her being able to keep the promises made.

15　THE COMPUTER WORLD　(Levels B & C)

This activity is in two parts:

PART ONE should be done as a class discussion to guide the
    thinking of the pupils;
PART TWO should be done as pair or small group work with one
    member of the group or pair writing down their ideas for
    reading out to the class at the end of the lesson.

PART ONE

The following suggestions can be used to lead the discussion on
computers and robots.

1   If you had unlimited money, which home computer would you
    like to possess, and why?

2   What do you consider the most important functions a home
    computer should be able to perform?
    (The teacher should write the suggestions on the board.)
    Now choose the top 5 functions and list them in order of
    importance (the final list should be arrived at by a consensus).

3   What do you think will be the 5 main things that a computer
    will be able to do to make life easier in the home of the future?
    (The teacher should list these on the board.)

4   Many people think the future home computers will be robots.
    Do you agree? Why, or why not?

5   What are the advantages and disadvantages a robot might have
    compared with a more conventional computer?

6   Do you think robots could ever become the enemy of human
    beings? What might happen? How could we avoid this?

PART TWO

Divide the pupils into groups to discuss and work on the following
situations. (One member of the group should write down an agreed
version to read to the class at the end of the lesson.)
    You may wish to have some groups discussing option 'A' and

others discussing option 'B'. It is also possible for all groups to work on both 'A' and 'B'.

OPTION A

A DAY IN THE LIFE OF MARVIN THE HOMEMAKER
Imagine you are Marvin.
An important magazine has asked you to send it a tape in which you discuss a typical 24-hour day, describing in detail your life in the home. Think of what will interest people; leave out obvious things like 'I get out of bed' and introduce your personal feelings about the events.

OPTION B

A DAY IN THE LIFE OF HAROLD THE SCHOOLMATE
Imagine you are Harold.
An important magazine has asked you to send it a tape describing a typical day at school.
There will be several types of lesson, and several teachers.
Remember to express your FEELINGS about what you enjoy, hate or endure.

16   THE IDEAL HOME   (Levels A, B & C)

This is an activity for group discussion on a domestic and very interesting subject.

1   Divide the class into small discussion groups and explain that they are going to try and come to an agreement on what they think would be the IDEAL HOME for the average Mr & Mrs BRITAIN.

2   Explain that the discussion will be done under various headings, which you will write on the board, as below.
     Allow about 10 minutes discussion, and then bring the groups together to pool their ideas and try to come to an agreement about this 'architect-designed' home of their imagination.

     HEADINGS

     a   *TYPE:* wooden, glass, plastic, brick etc.
               a cottage, in a block of flats, a bungalow etc.
               modern, 20, 50, 100, 200 years old etc.

     b   *SITUATION:* on a main road, by a river, on the 23rd floor of a city block etc.

     c   *INSIDE OF HOUSE:* how many rooms, which rooms etc.

     d   *GARDEN:* concrete yard, pool, lawn, trees, shrubs etc.

     e   *STYLE OF FURNITURE:* modern, antique etc.

3   Now explain to the groups that you will write on the board a list of appliances and devices and that Mr & Mrs Britain are permitted to have only 10 of them. Which 10 should these be? Have the groups list their choices in order of importance. (Allow 5 minutes discussion, and then bring the groups together to pool their ideas and try to come to a consensus.)

     APPLIANCES AND DEVICES (they already have a cooker and refrigerator)

washing machine	video	liquidiser	television
microwave oven	floor polisher	stereo	hair dryer
spin dryer	stainless steel sink	dishwasher	deep freeze
vacuum cleaner	food mixer	telephone	home computer

4   *WHAT ABOUT COLOURS?*

     Write the following lists of colours and criteria on the board and ask the groups to list the colours 1–6 according to each criterion. (Allow 6–8 minutes for discussion, and then pool the groups' ideas and discuss the decisions made.)

COLOURS: red violet green brown white blue

CRITERIA: restful cheerful cool warm useful stimulating

Have the pupils decide on the ideal colour scheme for Mr & Mrs Britain's home. (They may use colours not already mentioned in previous exercises.)

FOLLOW-UP

A   Ask the pupils to describe in a few sentences how they would spend a big sum of money they have just won, on making their *own* home more comfortable and beautiful.

B   The number of topics that can arise is obviously endless. For example, why is the cost of a 'personalised' house so high? What types of houses do people normally have to be content with, and what faults do they find?

VARIATION (Levels B & C)

People of different ages and types will have different ideas on what makes the ideal home. Choose one of the biographies below and have the groups discuss the various topics, 2–4, according to the specific information they now have on Mr & Mrs Britain.

i	Mr & Mrs Britain	retired couple, sociable, 2 grandchildren. Mrs Britain likes sewing, gardening, goldfish, painting. Mr Britain likes sport, woodwork, television.
ii	Mr & Mrs Britain	both are teachers in their 40's, 2 teenage children. Like entertaining at home. Mrs Britain is writing a book; Mr Britain is a TV fanatic.
iii	Mr & Mrs Britain	both are in their 20's, married 18 months ago, have a baby boy. Mrs Britain likes cooking, does typing at home. Mr Britain likes photography (does his own developing), and reading.

This activity is in 3 parts, and is best done as follows:

1   in groups of 4;

2   in pairs;

3   individually.

PART ONE

Divide the class into groups of about 4.
Make sure there is *an even number* of groups, even though some may not be 4s.
Label one half of the groups 'A' and the balancing half 'B'.
Have the groups discuss the following situations for 10–15 minutes.

GROUPS 'A'
It is the year 2086

Explain to the pupils that each group 'A' is a person who is famous throughout the world. The person may be a pop star, a scientist, a musician, a politician – any FAMOUS person at all. In the groups, they should choose who the person is going to be, and create a biography for him/her.
They should include such things as

– date and place of birth
– early life
– when and why he/she became famous
– likes and dislikes
– thoughts on world affairs
– hopes for the future
– a 'secret life' story

Each member of the group should write down the details agreed on as each member will act the part of the famous person in Part 2.

GROUPS 'B'

It is the same year – 2086

Explain to the pupils that each group in the 'B' half is a group of reporters for the local newspaper, 'The Echo'. They are being sent to interview a famous person who is visiting their town for one day.

In the groups they should work out the questions they think they should ask to get all the information they can about the visiting personality: e.g. In your home or school, Mr Racine, was there any one particular person who helped you towards success?

PART TWO

When both sets of groups are ready with their questions and information, pupils in groups 'A' should pair off with pupils in groups 'B' to conduct the interview. This should last about 5 minutes. Remind the interviewers that it is wise to start with easy, pleasant questions in order to put the interviewee at ease.

PART THREE

Once information has been gained, the pupils should return to their seats to write up their findings. Pupils from groups 'A' should write out *'a day in the life of'* the personality they represent, to be printed in 'The Echo's' Sunday edition.

Pupils from groups 'B' should write a scoop article for 'The Echo' on the visiting personality – including the headline, e.g.

FAMOUS AUTHOR GETS HIS IDEAS FROM DREAMS

The work can be displayed for all to enjoy.

This activity is best done in small groups.

Explain to the class that one of the big decisions that the pupils will have to make in life is what they will do with themselves after their schooling is over.

This activity will look at how to decide what job to choose.

1   Divide the class into small discussion groups.
Write the following list of jobs on the board.
Ask the pupils to see if they can write a brief but accurate description of three of them, which would include what the person does in the job.

a disc-jockey	a secretary
a solicitor	a radio operator on a ship
a model	a policeman
an air hostess	a nurse
an estate agent	a shop assistant
an airline pilot	an engineer

Allow 10 minutes for discussion, then have each group in turn give you one definition. See if other groups agree, and encourage them to improve on the explanation.

2   Now explain to the groups that certain jobs are best done when the workers have certain qualities or personalities. Ask the pupils to give you as many *good points* in a person's character as possible. Write these on the board as they are fired at you.
You might begin with CHARM, HONESTY, ACCURACY, PATIENCE. ... (use only *half* the board; label this *LIST A*).

3   Now ask each group to give you 2–3 jobs people do – for example BUS DRIVER, ENGINEER, POTTER. Write these on the board and label them *LIST B*.

4   Have the groups discuss the lists to find for each of the jobs
    presented in List B, the *5 most important qualities* from List A that
    are needed to be a successful worker in each of the jobs. The
    groups should list these qualities 1–5 in order of importance to
    the job.
    Allow about 15 minutes for the discussion.

5   Finally, have the pupils report their findings back to the class as
    a whole.
    Discuss these and try to come to a consensus.

6   If time allows, try to stimulate a discussion on the nature of
    UNUSUAL JOBS, and how people get into them e.g.

an inspector of sewers

a zoo keeper/assistant

a vivisectionist ... plenty of argument will follow!

a thatcher

a radiographer

a restorer of antique furniture

a ceramic artist

a saggar-maker's bottom knocker (!)

a steeplejack

a diver

Solve this One

Problem solving

---

19 SURVIVAL (Levels A, B & C)

---

1   Divide the class into discussion groups, of not more than 5. (A small enough group to discuss quietly round a small table.)

2   Set the scene as follows:
Imagine you have been a passenger in an aeroplane which has crashed into a mountain 2000 metres high. You have escaped with only shock and minor burns. There is snow all around you. From amongst the wreckage you find the following items. Number them in order of necessity for your survival (1 is the most important, 15 the least important).

     a box of matches

     signal flares

     first aid kit

     parachute

     three wooden cases of dehydrated milk

     25 litres of fresh water

     a life-jacket

50 metres of nylon rope

a map of the mountain area

a bottle of whisky

an inflatable raft

a pair of sunglasses

3 woollen blankets

a battery-run transistor radio

an army-knife

(This list can be written on the board)

3   Give the groups 20 minutes for discussion.

4   When they have decided on their orders of priority, bring the groups back together for the feedback session. The aim is to try and come to a general definitive solution after comparing the results of the groups and discussing the differences. The discussion will be tidier if a speaker for each group is elected to lead for the group. The others do not have to remain silent; they will want to reinforce their representative's points from time to time. As there is no one correct answer, any sensible solution should be accepted so long as all possible uses of the individual items have been understood, e.g. the parachute could be used to build a shelter.

The following might also be considered by the different levels.

LEVEL A

You have gone fishing and your boat has drifted out to sea out of sight of land. You have:

a box of matches

oars

an oil-lamp with oil

binoculars

a fisherman's knife

a lifebelt

string

a bottle of water

a small sail, and mast

a compass

fish-hooks and fishing rod

a book

a pencil

some chocolate

a bucket

LEVEL C

You are with an expedition exploring at the North Pole. You
have become separated from your companions by a snowstorm.
You have:

a small sledge

a 5 litre can of water (frozen)

a tin of sardines

a first aid kit

a box of matches

a pair of sunglasses

a Husky to pull the sledge

a magnetic compass

a camper's stove and gas

30 metres of rope

2 flares

a bottle of brandy

a sleeping-bag

a stretcher

a hunting-knife

a car battery

a radio receiver

The lists can either be dictated, or displayed on the board.

---

20 PICTOGRAMS (Levels A, B & C)

This is an activity for individuals, pairs or small groups. The pupils will enjoy pitting their wits against others', and they will be asked to bring into play their powers of encoding and decoding.

At Level A the messsage may be short and simple.

At Level C there may be more complex words to deal with and longer messages may be expected.

Essentially, the activity involves the displaying of a message in picture form as follows.

1   Each picture may represent a whole word

e.g.   (ewe) = you

or a part of a word

e.g.   8 Oh Oh   (pot eight Ohs) = potatoes

2   New letters may be substituted for those not required

e.g.   ɓ L   (bike − b = ike + L) = like

3   Letters at the beginning and end of a word may be removed

e.g.   (cat − c) = at

56

An enjoyable competitive element may be introduced by asking the pupils to write messages for other groups to decode and answer.

For all levels, correct spelling of the decoded message is essential.

To provide inspiration the following could be used as examples:

21 HETTY HIGGINS (Levels A, B & C)

This game aims to have fun with spelling, and to test the pupils' powers of deduction.

As the name of the game suggests, words containing *double letters* are the ones to be considered (though there are other categories of words that can be used as well).

Have the pupils seated in a rough circle so that they can take turns to speak in an orderly manner. Include yourself in this circle. Set the scene as follows:

> We are going to discuss a very strange girl called Hetty Higgins. She is strange because she likes an odd combination of things, and sometimes seems to contradict herself when she says she likes one thing but doesn't like another. For example, she likes *sweets* but doesn't like *chocolate*, and she likes *looking* at TV but doesn't like *watching* it. I want each of you to try and work out what kinds of things Hetty likes by a process of elimination. Each of you in turn will say, "Hetty Higgins likes … x … but doesn't like … y …" If you have chosen the correct likes and dislikes I will say, "yes." If you haven't made the right choice, I will say, "no." You may choose anything you like. At first you will have to guess what Hetty likes but, if you really think about the

things which I say are correct, you should soon know the types of things to say.

When you think you have found the clue to Hetty's strange habits, DON'T tell anyone what the answer is. Simply continue, when it is your turn, to say the correct things. Let's see how good your detective powers are.

Begin the game yourself:

Hetty Higgins likes *cabbage* but doesn't like *tomatoes*. The pupil next to you in a clockwise direction should then try, and so on round the class. If a pupil is not successful, don't pause or have a post mortem – continue with the next pupil so that the words that are required are deduced by the players from the examples given in the correct statements.

Try and keep the pace moving – don't allow more than a couple of seconds for thinking.

The game has no set time limit – it can continue till the last pupil has found the key.

OTHER POSSIBILITIES

1   HETTY HIGGINS likes words with 2 syllables only.

e.g. Hetty Higgins likes *papers* but not *magazines*.
    Hetty Higgins likes to *begin* things, but not to *end* them.

2   STEPHEN STALKER (a cousin of Hetty) likes words with silent letters including: final silent R; silent K as in knee; and foreign words: restaurant; ballet.

e.g. Stephen Stalker likes to chee*r*, but not to shout.
    Stephen Stalker likes *k*nowledge, but not information.
    Stephen Stalker likes ha*l*ves, but not seconds.

This activity can be done individually, in pairs, or in small groups.

a   Write the following *logic wheels* and *magic squares* on the board.

b   Have the pupils copy them down and use their detective powers to find the missing letters.

1

? M
A   O
G   I
E K

2

? Z
   W
H
  N S

3

C	G	K
G	M	N
K	S	?

4

A	F	K
J	O	T
M	R	?

5

? A
I   B
E C

6

? A
O   C
J F

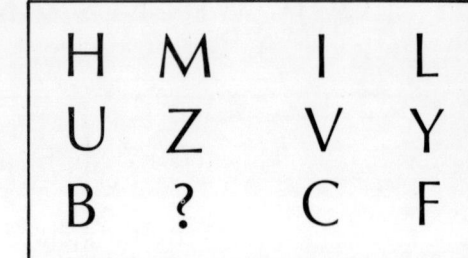

7

Y	V		X	W
O	I		M	K
T	K		Q	?

8

H	M		I	L
U	Z		V	Y
B	?		C	F

ANSWERS 1 C; 2 A; 3 Q; 4 W; 5 Q; 6 U; 7 N; 8 G

FOLLOW-UP ACTIVITIES

c   Have the pupils create their own logic wheels and magic squares.

d   Take *logic wheel 1 or magic square 4* and have the pupils see how many words can be made from the letters there.

23   THE PUBLICITY CAMPAIGN
(Levels A, B & C)

Divide the class into groups of four pupils, then set the scene as follows:

Your local council has a problem. It would like to spend money on an advertising campaign to promote your area as a tourist attraction, but it is not sure to which agency to give the job. Therefore, a competition has been announced to find out which agency can offer the best advertisements.

Two things must be submitted:

1   a pamphlet;

2   a script for a short TV advertisement.

Each group is an agency in the competition.

1   Ask the pupils to tell you what they think makes up a good
     advertisement.
     Write up on the board the suggestions they give you.
     The following 6 points will help to get the discussion going.

     1   It catches the eye and/or attention.

     2   It holds the attention.

     3   It is not too long.

     4   It is easy to remember.

     5   It praises the good qualities/discourages the bad elements.

     6   It encourages the listener/reader/viewer to do something
          about it.

2   Have the pupils plan their campaigns carefully. They should
     discuss in their groups what should be in the pamphlet and in
     the TV programme. For example, should the latter be an
     interview, or a jingle to go with a series of pictures of the area?
     They should also decide on a division of labour – perhaps 2 to
     do the pamphlet and 2 to do the TV programme.

3   Have the pupils prepare their exhibits to be displayed at the end
     of the lesson.
     As you are among the groups while they are working, you are
     bound to discover one or two outstanding 'productions' of the
     TV interview. Try to leave time at the end of the lesson for at
     least 2 of these to be performed to the class.

OTHER SUGGESTIONS

     End pollution of the countryside

     The police are your friends

     Every family should own a computer

     School lunches should be free

     Your new pedestrian precinct

     Don't go home with a stranger

     Your local theatre needs publicity

This activity is best done in pairs, or in small groups.

Explain that a group of people of widely different types is to be arranged in a way that will create the least friction among them. It is therefore important to take into account each person's different limitations, relationships and individual quirks.

There is not necessarily *one* correct answer. Any sensible and defensible layout can be accepted. A compromise is usually the best solution.

1   Divide the pupils into pairs or small discussion groups and ask them to appoint a group leader.

2   Explain the problem as follows:

You are the Social Committee for your town/area and have organised a day's outing – a mystery coach trip – to be sponsored by a local firm.

Enough people have said they will come to enable you to fill a minibus but, on examination of the passenger list, you find you have a very varied group of people. From the biographies I shall put on the board, sort out the seating plan which you think will ensure that everyone has a good chance of enjoying the day. The bus seats 14 people:

    5 at the back;
    2 rows of 2 on each side;
    1 near the driver.

Allow about 20 minutes for the discussion. Ask each group to draw a plan of the seating and to put in the names.

3   In the *FEEDBACK SESSION* the group leaders should write their proposals on the board for comparison, discussion and possible adjustment in the light of the other groups' ideas. It is helpful if you guide the groups to remind them of all the implications of the problem. You can also offer other combinations for the different groups to think about. They must also explain – and argue about – the reasons for their allocation of seats.

BIOGRAPHIES (to be written on the board for use during the discussion)

Sue aged 25   Well-educated, sociable, ambitious, hard-working.

Paul aged 24   Aggressive, unemployed, in and out of prison.

John aged 18   Unemployed and can't find work, sociable, lively.

Pam aged 20   Hippy, talkative, not well-educated, a drifter.

Bill aged 40   Successful businessman, loud, boasts about money and properties.

Jackie aged 50 Hard-of-hearing, talkative but repeats herself, talks about her family and the war.

Mark aged 16   Shy, quiet, polite.

Jill aged 17   Noisy, overpowering personality.

Jim aged 34   Family died in a car accident, withdrawn, suicidal.

Siz aged 19   Punk, dyed hair, sociable, talks loudly about nothing.

Katy aged 47   A matron in the local hospital, friendly but stern and bossy.

Henry aged 27 Social worker, lively, cheerful, chatty, likes sorting out people's problems.

Lisa aged 40   Secretary, reserved, prim and proper.

James aged 41 Teacher of English, bossy, know-all, talkative.

There is one separate single seat. How many students would allocate that seat to the loner, Jim?

ALTERNATIVE

You have organised a mystery tour by bus for your class. Arrange the seating plan so that everyone will enjoy the trip.

(Levels A, B & C)

PART ONE of this activity should be done in small discussion groups.
PART TWO should be done by individuals.

PART ONE

Divide the pupils into groups and explain that this year is a special anniversary year for Nobel Prizes. The groups represent the Prize Committee whose job is to choose the winners. This year, it has been decided to award a special prize to the candidate thought to have done the most for other people. The committee must choose from the following list of finalists (which should be written on the board).

Princess Anne, Pope John Paul II, Bob Geldof, Mother Theresa, Mahatma Gandhi, Henri Dunant (founder of the Red Cross), Florence Nightingale, The United Nations Organisation, Louis Braille

First spend a few minutes making sure that the students understand who or what these people and organisations are, then have the pupils discuss which candidate should receive the Anniversary Medal.

If a candidate is now dead, the medal will be presented to the Mayor of the candidate's home town.

When their choices have been made, the groups should prepare short speeches which will be read out at the presentation ceremony, explaining to the world why their successful finalists were chosen. Allow 10–15 minutes for discussion and preparation of the speeches – they should be *written*, at least in note form, but preferably in full text.

Bring the groups together to discuss the choices and present the speeches.

PART TWO

Now, have each pupil imagine he/she is the chairperson of the committee and thus can award his/her own 'Chairperson's Nobel

Prize'. Each pupil should, therefore, choose his/her hero or heroine – anyone from the beginning of time to the present day – who should be recognised as the greatest person who has ever lived on earth.

Have *each pupil* prepare a short speech which could be read out at the presentation ceremony. The award will be presented to the Mayor of the home town of the person chosen.

Allow about 10 minutes for this section, and finish the lesson with one or two selections from the individual choices and speeches.

AN ALTERNATIVE CRITERION FOR PART ONE

This year it has been decided to award a special prize for the greatest contribution to *SCIENCE*. The committee must choose from the following list of finalists, which you should write on the board:

Clive Sinclair, Alexander Bell, Marie Curie, Thomas Edison, John Logie Baird, Louis Pasteur, Ernest Rutherford

Again, it will first be necessary to make sure that the pupils know exactly for what each person is famous (Chambers Biographical Dictionary – almost certainly in the school library – is the ideal reference book here).

Everyone's a Writer

Poetry and short story writing

26   THE KITE   (Levels A, B & C)

Writing accurately demands precision of thought and discipline in putting ideas down on paper. (But you may need to explain that in simpler terms.)

KITE-FLYING is a form of writing which encourages such discipline. It is best done individually by members of the class.

The exercise involves the pupils counting the number of syllables in each line they write and building up a structure with the following pattern

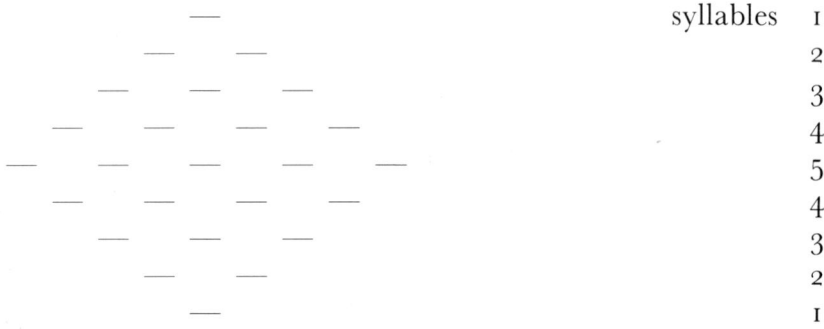

	syllables	1
		2
		3
		4
		5
		4
		3
		2
		1

The number of syllables per line starts with one and increases progressively to 5. It then decreases again to one. The 5-syllable line may contain one word of 5 syllables, 5 words of one syllable, or any other combination adding up to 5.

As an introduction to the exercise, give the pupils a topic such as *SUNRISE* and ask them to give you all the words that they associate with the topic – colours, sights, sounds, movement. Write these on the board. Do not spend more than 3 or 4 minutes doing this.

Then, together with the pupils, fly your kites. Concentrate on one aspect only of a sunrise.

e.g.

one

ball of

pulsating

vibrant orange

balances on the

grey tightrope that

holds apart

sea and

sky

Now, ask the pupils to choose their own subjects.

Get them to write down their own lists of words associated with the ideas and then encourage them to fly their own kites.

For those who have difficulty choosing a topic, the following suggestions might help.

The cat	e.g. My	1
Waterfall	Persian	2
The Storm	green-eyed Tom	3
The Old Man	meticulous	4
Night	in his cleanliness	5
	sits washing to	4
	perfection	3
	pale grey	2
	paws	1

They will find, after the first attempt, that it is not difficult at all.

This exercise is best done individually.

The haiku is a traditional form of Japanese verse which introduces the concept of *rhythm* in words. It encourages economy of statement, and a concentration on one aspect of the topic chosen. Pupils of all ages and abilities enjoy the challenge of precision of thought that is required.

It is composed of 3 short lines of 5, 7 and 5 syllables respectively, a total of 17 syllables overall.

. . . . 5 syllables

. . . . 7 syllables

. . . . 5 syllables

As an introduction, you might like to work through an example with the class. In this way the process of 'polishing' to find just the right words and rhythms can be demonstrated, e.g.

THE TREE

Living umbrella,

Open against the downpour

Protecting the earth.

Now encourage the pupils to choose their own subjects. For those who find it hard to start, the following suggestions could be given.

School	Christmas
War	Dreams
A Rose	Fear
Goldfish	The Tortoise
Computers	A Frog

This is a class activity which could later be repeated in pairs or small groups.

If words are carefully combined, powerful moods can be created, and pictures painted in the mind.

As a class exercise, under your guidance, paint a picture by playing with the rhythms and images inherent in words, and working for powerful effects. This is not difficult as long as a brisk working pace is maintained.

1   Ask 3 or 4 pupils at random to give you *a noun*.
    Write the suggestions quickly on the board as they are given to you.

2   Ask the class to choose the one suggestion which looks the most interesting. Rub out the others and rewrite the chosen noun, in title form, at the top of the board.

3   *Now have a brainstorming session.*
    Ask the pupils to fire at you any words and short phrases they can think of which are connected with the chosen topic. Write these on the board, leaving about $\frac{1}{3}$ of the board free for the final stage. Fill the space with suggestions. You will have to use a veto on ideas which cannot be depended on as having connections with the topic.

4   With the pupils' help, select the words which fit together in a natural or exciting way and thus which can be used to 'paint a picture' of your topic.
    Write them up in verse form, working for rhythm, flow of words, and picturesque ideas.

For Example: CAT

violent	twitching	night huntress	midnight prowler
playful	darting	amber-eyed	chases
purring	melting into darkness	whiskers	rushing out
sleeper	watchman	soft	undercover
		murderess	winsome

Amber-eyed huntress
Long-whiskered and soft,
Melting into darkness
On the midnight watch;
Darting out from cover
In the rush of violent chase,
Then winsome and purring,
The twitching murderess sleeps.

5   Divide the pupils into pairs or small groups. Have them repeat
the process on their own.
Display the finished work for all to share. There will be some
surprisingly good results.

29 A SOLDIER'S TALE (Level C only)

This is an exercise in guided writing. The pupils will work
individually and will need writing materials.

You will read the pupils the instructions set out below which they
must follow *exactly*. A reasonable time for writing should be allowed
between each step. Each set of instructions will need to be repeated at
least twice.

As a result of the exercise, each pupil will have an original piece of
writing on the theme of DULCE ET DECORUM EST by
Wilfred Owen. (You will have to translate later. DULCE ET
DECORUM EST PRO PATRIA MORI – It is sweet and
seemly to die for one's country.)

The poem is reproduced at the end for reading to the class, and
possibly for discussion by the pupils should time permit. The pupils
might consider such things as:

a   the choices of titles for the poem, and their own
contributions;

b   a comparison of their adjectives and descriptive phrases with
those of Owen;

c   whether or not they consider the poem would have had
more impact if it had been written as a story.

THE EXERCISE

We are going to build up a picture in writing according to some instructions I shall give you.

Listen carefully to the scenes I describe, and then write down what you would like to say about them in the number of lines I give you. Sometimes you will need to write only 1 line, sometimes 3 or 4.

1   Imagine you and your comrades are a group of soldiers on a muddy battlefield. You have been fighting for many months, and are so exhausted you can't stand straight. You are all sick with chest complaints, and cough as you move around in the mud. In *2 lines* describe the group of soldiers. Remember, you are one of the men.

2.   You are trying to march away from the front line, back to safety and some rest. You leave the bursting shells and flares of the battle behind you.
Describe this in *2 lines*.

3   You describe the men more exactly now.
They appear too tired to think or to see where they are marching. Many have lost their boots, and have cuts on their feet. It is painful to walk. All of them are so very tired that they move like drunken men and don't even hear the sound of the gas-shells which begin to fall behind them.
Use *4 lines* for your description.

4   *EMERGENCY!*
You suddenly realise that you are surrounded by *poisonous gas*. Shout a warning to the others in the group.
Use *1 line* only.

5   Even though you are all exhausted, you use all the speed you can muster to put on the awkward gas masks you carry in your kits. Most of you are successful, but one man is too slow and staggers about, crying out as the gas gets into his lungs.
Describe the scene in *3 lines*.

6   The gas is thick now, a greenish pea-soup colour. It is difficult to

see your comrades through these ghastly clouds.
In *2 lines* describe the scene.

7   You will never forget seeing your comrade come rushing towards
     you through the gas. You feel totally helpless in the situation as
     the gas gets into his lungs and he coughs horribly. You know he
     is going to die.
     Describe this in *2 lines*.

8   You are so disgusted by what you see and hear that you now try
     to involve your readers in your experience. You ask your readers
     directly to imagine what they would feel like to have to walk
     behind the wagon carrying the victim and to watch the man
     writhing and dying in agony.
     Use *4 lines* to do this. Include a brief description of what the
     dying man looks like.

9   In *4 lines* ask the readers to imagine what it would be like to
     have to listen to the dying man as the movement of the wagon
     across the uneven ground forces the blood up from his lungs,
     which are now being turned into blood and mucus by the gas.

10   In your last *4 lines* you want to tell the readers that if they had
     experienced what you have described, they wouldn't wish to say
     ever again that it is *glorious* to die for your country.
     Say this in any way you feel.

11   Give a title to what you have written.

12   Now read the poem slowly to the class.

Dulce et Decorum Est

Bent double, like old beggars under sacks,
Knock-kneed, coughing like hags, we cursed through sludge,
Till on the haunting flares we turned our backs,
And towards our distant rest began to trudge.
Men marched asleep. Many had lost their boots,
But limped on, blood-shod. All went lame, all blind;
Drunk with fatigue; deaf even to the hoots
Of gas-shells dropping softly behind.

Gas! Gas! Quick, boys! – An ecstasy of fumbling,
Fitting the clumsy helmets just in time,
But someone still was yelling out and stumbling
And floundering like a man in fire or lime. –
Dim through the misty panes and thick green light,
As under a green sea, I saw him drowning.

In all my dreams before my helpless sight
He plunges at me, guttering, choking, drowning.

If in some smothering dreams, you too could pace
Behind the wagon that we flung him in,
And watch the white eyes writhing in his face,
His hanging face, like a devil's sick of sin;
If you could hear, at every jolt, the blood
Come gargling from the froth-corrupted lungs,
Bitter as the cud
Of vile, incurable sores on innocent tongues, –
My friend, you would not tell with such high zest
To children ardent for some desperate glory,
The old Lie: Dulce et decorum est
Pro patria mori.

30   THE INCREDIBLE JOURNEY
(Levels A, B & C)

For this exercise, the pupils can work individually, in pairs, or in
small groups of up to 4.

The activity involves using a series of incongruous elements to write
a short story about a journey. *All* the elements that are given should
be included in the story in the order and form in which they are
presented.

On the board, write out the whole set of elements for the class as a
whole. If everyone is working on the same set of stimuli, the different
results will be a source of entertainment when the stories are read to

the other members of the class at the end of the lesson.

The exercise can be lengthened by the addition of an extra word just when the pupils think they have completed the task.

The following are examples of sets of incongruous elements that could be used.

LEVEL A

1   tiger, television, joyful, tulip field, dance, lemonade

2   the Prime Minister, motorway, key, banana, laugh, shakily, "where am I?"

3   actress, aunt, nose, alligator, motionless, paddle, as fast as possible

Example No. 1

> Now you may think it very strange that a young *tiger* should have a *television* set; but the reason is that he never knew he was a tiger. When he was very young indeed, in fact just after he was born, he was found in the long grass by a man who was hunting. So the first living thing the tiger ever saw was this man; this made the young tiger think he too was a human being. He was taken to a house next to a huge *tulip field* and lived with the family. When they watched TV he watched TV. If they could *dance* he could dance – just like any human, only better. When they drank *lemonade*, he drank lemonade. Not that he liked it much, but if they did it he had to do it too. In fact it was a very *joyful* life . . . until the tiger began to grow up. Then he felt quite different .'. . and you can imagine what happened next.

There is a deliberate error in the construction of that 'story'. In what way does it not keep to the rules given?

LEVEL B

1   electronic, skate, greasy, explosively, Napoleon, nail varnish, rhinoceros

2   microbe, jungle, telephone, snowflake, religiously, potato

3   elephant, matchbox, vegetarian, double bass, ventriloquist, bride

Example No. 3

Of course it's very difficult to imagine why an *elephant* and a *matchbox* should come into the same story, but they did. Actually, the animal ate the matchbox – he liked wooden things to eat anyway, being a *vegetarian* (I mean, who has ever seen an elephant eating meat?), and actually it was the musician playing the *double bass* who had thrown it to him during a break in the music. Music, you ask? Why music at the zoo? Well, it was a strange day; never anything like it before. A party of people came with this orchestra, all beautifully dressed, especially the ladies. One was all in white, with a veil. The elephant found it very strange, especially when he heard the lady chattering like a monkey. The wedding party was led by a *ventriloquist*, you see, and he thought it funny to get the *bride* to make these zoo noises, even though he was the bridegroom. The elephant was not amused.

LEVEL C

1   fashion model, Garden of Eden, fossil, congratulate, crocodile, Neil Armstrong, "how are you?"

2   needle-like, atmosphere, obstruction, inner city, daisy, silicon chip, Siberia, "but it's not cricket"

3   detective, moon crater, Cleopatra, shark, chocolate cake, gloves, "let's dance"

Example No. 2

Sarah felt as soon as she entered the room a sharp, almost *needle-like* sensation of pain; not a physical pain but an intense and sudden sensation of dislike. Eyes upon her showed distaste. The *atmosphere* was hateful. Here, at once she knew, she would find nothing but *obstruction* to the plans she hoped to explain. That was what *inner city* life did to people; made them distrustful and hateful. People brought up among blocks of concrete had never known grass, or streams, or noted the beauty of a *daisy*, or the delight of a nightingale's song. People spent their days talking about stocks and shares and the *silicon chip*, and growled about the Russian menace, the KGB and the hell of prison in *Siberia*. And if someone did something mean they muttered, "Oh, *but it's not cricket*, old boy!" as though meanness, dishonesty and the disasters of politics were just a game.

Sarah knew without saying a word that they would never really listen. She turned on her heel and abruptly left.

31 DENOUEMENTS (Levels A, B & C)

This is an exercise which involves the writing of a story by a *series* of authors. It is important, therefore, that handwriting is neat and clear so that the whole story can be read aloud easily by anyone at the end of the exercise.

The activity works best if done individually, or in pairs.

The aim is to produce a story in 4 paragraphs, written in sequence by 4 different people. It is important that none of the writers knows what has been written before he or she adds his/her contribution. The consequences of this are often very amusing, sometimes very clever, and occasionally brilliant – even informative!

INSTRUCTIONS

Take a sheet of paper and fold it in half from top to bottom. Repeat the folding process so that your sheet should now be divided into 4 horizontal sections, not 4 quarters.

SECTION 1 In the first section, *using not more than 50 words, SET THE SCENE* for the story. Try and create an exciting atmosphere, but only set the scene. Do not make anything dramatic happen to anyone. You

could begin with, 'It was a cold, misty night out-side. But inside was warm and cosy, but spooky . . .' (Allow 4–5 minutes for the writing.)
Now fold the first section backwards so that what you have written cannot be seen. Hand your sheet to the person on your right.

SECTION 2   In the second section, *using not more than 50 words, DESCRIBE A PERSON* – anyone you like.
Try and describe the person accurately – the face, clothes, movements, actions and even feelings.
(Allow 4–5 minutes for the writing.)
Now fold the second section backwards so that both sections 1 and 2 can't be seen.
Hand the sheet to the person on your right.

SECTION 3   In the third section, *using not more than 50 words* again, *DESCRIBE SOMETHING THAT HAPPENED* – a football match goal, a wedding, a murder, a street accident, an unexpected meeting with someone.
(Allow 4–5 minutes for the writing.)
Now fold the third section over backwards as you did for sections 1 and 2.
Pass the sheet to the person on your right.

SECTION 4   In the fourth section, *using not more than 50 words, DESCRIBE THE CONSEQUENCES* of what you think happened in the section 3 you have now.
(Allow 4–5 minutes for the writing.)

Collect all the papers, shuffle them, and distribute them to the members of the class to read aloud.

OTHER SUGGESTIONS FOR STORIES *(using not more than 50 words* per section)

a   Section 1   Describe a place where something has happened.

2 Describe a person moving in a special way in an area or place. (Include the reason why the person moves in this way.)

3 'Suddenly he/she saw . . .'
Describe what was seen, what it looked like, what it was doing.

4 Describe what the person did about it.

b Section 1 Write a paragraph starting, 'As the spacecraft rose off the launching pad . . .'

2 Write a paragraph starting, 'Suddenly I found . . .'

3 Write a paragraph starting, 'We were obviously on our way to . . .'

4 Write a paragraph starting, 'There was only one answer . . .'

32 UNLIKELY ORIGINS (Levels A, B & C)

This is an activity for individual work.

Charles Lamb, a writer who lived from 1775 to 1834, once tried to explain in a humorous way the origins of roast pork in the following story. Listen while I read it.

1 Read aloud the story:

How we got Roast Pork

Mankind, says a Chinese manuscript, for the first seventy thousand ages ate their meat raw. The art of roasting, was accidentally discovered in the following manner. The swine-herd, Ho-ti, having gone out into the woods one morning, as his manner was, to collect food for his hogs, left his cottage in the care of his eldest son Bo-bo, a great lubberly boy, who being fond of playing with fire, as children of his age commonly are, let some sparks escape into a bundle of straw, which kindling quickly, spread the conflagration over every part of their poor mansion, till it was reduced to ashes. Together with the cottage, what was of much more importance, a fine litter of new-farrowed pigs, no less than nine in number, perished. China pigs have been thought a luxury all over the East from the remotest periods that we read of. Bo-bo was in the utmost consternation, as you may think, not so much for the sake of the tenement, which his father and he could easily build up again with a few dry branches, and the labour of an hour or two, at any time, as for the loss of the pigs. While he was thinking what he should say to his father, and wringing his hands over the smoking remnants of one of those untimely sufferers, an odour assailed his nostrils, unlike any scent which he had before experienced. What could it proceed from? – not from the burnt cottage – he had smelt that smell before – indeed this was by no means the first accident of the kind which had occurred through the negligence of this unlucky young fire-brand. Much less did it resemble that of any known herb, weed, or flower. He knew not what to think. He next stooped down to feel the pig, if there were any signs of life in it. He burnt his fingers, and to cool them he applied them in his booby fashion to his mouth. Some of the crumbs of the scorched skin had come away with his fingers, and for the first time in his life (in the world's life indeed, for before him no man had known it) he tasted – *crackling!* Again he felt and fumbled at the pig. It did not burn him so much now, still he licked his fingers from a sort of habit. The truth at length broke into his slow understanding, that it was the pig that smelt so, and the pig that tasted so delicious; and, surrendering himself up to the newborn pleasure, he fell to tearing up whole handfuls of the scorched skin with the flesh next it, and was cramming it down his throat when his father entered amid the smoking rafters, armed with retributory cudgel, and finding how affairs stood, began to rain blows upon the young rogue's shoulders, as thick as hailstones, which Bo-bo heeded not any more than if they had been flies. His father might lay on, but he could not beat him from his pig.

'You graceless whelp. Is it not enough that you have burnt down three houses with your dog's tricks, but you must be eating fire, and I know not what – what have you got there, I say?'

'O, father, the pig, the pig, do come and taste how nice the burnt pig is.'

The ears of Ho-ti tingled with horror. He cursed his son, and he cursed himself that ever he should beget a son that should eat burnt pig.

Bo-bo, whose scent was wonderfully sharpened since morning, soon raked out another pig, still shouting out 'Eat, eat, eat the burnt pig, father, only taste – O Lord.'

Ho-ti trembled in every joint while he grasped the abominable thing, wavering whether he should not put his son to death for an unnatural young monster, when the crackling scorching his fingers, as it had done his son's, and applying the same remedy to them, he in his turn tasted some of its flavour, which, make what sour mouths he would for a pretence, proved not altogether displeasing to him. In conclusion (for the manuscript here is a little tedious) both father and son promptly sat down to the meal, and never left off till they had despatched all that remained of the litter.

So, the discovery that the flesh of swine, or indeed of any other animal, might be cooked, was made.

(Adapted from A DISSERTATION UPON ROAST PIG: ESSAYS OF ELIA, Charles Lamb)

2   Ask the class for their critical comments. You could lead with the following questions:

   a   Do you think it is a true story? How can you tell?

   b   What caused the father to change his violent attitude to his 'graceless whelp' Bo-bo?

   c   Do you think that Charles Lamb enjoyed writing the story? What made you think so?

   d   Is roast pork your favourite 'roast'? or what?

3   Explain to the class that you are going to give them a name of something in our lives which is very common and which we often take for granted.
     Ask them to see if they can write a very short story (say 200 words) to explain its origin, and how it came to have its name. Here are some suggestions:

GROUP A	GROUP B	GROUP C
Reading glasses	A padlock	Language
A calendar	A calendar	A napkin ring
A table	Paper napkins	A calendar
Language	A comb	The wheel
The wheel	A clock	Gloves
Crisps	A fork	A ballpoint pen
A window frame	Cheese	Cornflakes
A doughnut	Trousers	An umbrella
An umbrella	An umbrella	A watch
A cupboard	Sunglasses	A shaver

4   The story of Charles Lamb's life is also worth telling: a remarkable story of a man's devotion to (and sacrifice for) his mentally sick sister; their initial poverty and their ultimate successes as writers and dramatists. In spite of all his personal troubles, Lamb still possessed a sense of humour, as the Roast Pig passage demonstrates.

33   FACT OR FABLE?   (Levels A, B & C)

This is an activity for individual work.

A fable can be described as a story in which creatures or inanimate objects act and speak like human beings, showing the same feelings and emotions as we do. It teaches us the difference between right and wrong, or how we ought to live our lives.

Listen to this fable which some of you may have heard before.

1   Read aloud:

Brer Rabbit, the Elephant and the Whale

'Yes,' said the elephant to Brer Rabbit, 'I don't think anyone would deny that I am the strongest creature on earth. Look how big I am.' And he drew himself up to his full height and raised his trunk in the air like a boxer who has just scored a knockout. 'I hope you don't think I'm boasting,' he went on. 'If you're as powerful as I am you can't help knowing it, any more than if you're a timid, feeble creature like you you can avoid knowing it.' He laughed unpleasantly.

Brer Rabbit laughed too, but he was not amused. 'My friend, don't be misled by your size,' he said. 'I know you can do a few party tricks like tearing up a tree by the roots, but you have no real strength – nothing to compare with my mighty muscles.' He sat up on his hind legs and drew in a deep breath to swell his tiny chest.

The elephant laughed so hard that he had to lean against a tree to save himself from falling. 'Your mighty muscles!' he choked. 'Oh dear, what a little comic you are!'

'I'm deadly serious,' said Brer Rabbit, 'and I'll prove it. Let's have a tug-o'-war. You take one end of this rope and I'll take the other. We'll see who can pull hardest.'

'This is ridiculous,' said the elephant, 'but I'll do it anyway. It'll teach you a lesson, you foolish little thing.'

Brer Rabbit tied the end of a long rope around the elephant's waist. 'Now I'll take the other end down on to the sands, through those bushes,' said Brer Rabbit. 'When I shout "Pull" do your worst.' The elephant agreed, Brer Rabbit tied the rope round him, and went off through the bushes on to the beach.

Not far out in the water a whale was sunning himself. 'Hello,' shouted Brer Rabbit, 'wasn't it you who told me yesterday that you were the strongest creature on earth?'

'It was,' answered the whale, 'but I don't suppose it was any news to you. I believe it's widely known.'

'I think I'm stronger than you,' said Brer Rabbit, 'and I'm ready to prove it. Let's have a tug-o'-war to see who's the tougher. I'll tie this rope around your waist and take the other end through the bushes up on to the grass. When I shout "Pull" pull. Okay?'

'Okay,' said the whale, hardly able to believe what he heard. Brer Rabbit tied the end of the rope round the great middle of the whale and went back up into the bushes. Once there he could not keep himself from laughing at the idea of the elephant at one end of the rope and the whale at the other. Then he shouted, 'Pull.'

The elephant gave a gentle tug. Nothing happened. He planted his great feet in the grass and gave a hefty pull. The whale was yanked his own length through the water.

'Cor!' he said, 'This little bloke isn't as feeble as he looks. I'll have to teach him a lesson.' With a powerful thrashing of his mighty tail he headed out to sea. The elephant found himself dragged off his feet and sliding along the grass on his bottom. He managed to slither to his feet and dug them into the ground to avoid being pulled into the sea. Then slowly he inched his way back from the bushes, where Brer Rabbit was lying chuckling at the groans and grunts of the two sweating giants. The whale felt himself slipping back towards the shore. He too exerted all his enormous strength. The great beasts strained at the rope until each was on the verge of collapse.

Brer Rabbit saw his chance. He shouted to the elephant, 'I could keep this up all day. Do you want to give up?'

'Yes,' gasped the elephant, falling gratefully on the grass.

Brer Rabbit turned towards the sea. 'Want to give up?' he shouted.

'I surrender,' panted the whale, as he sank to the bottom for a rest. As Brer Rabbit untied the rope from the defeated beasts he had the same message for each: 'Pride comes before a fall and boasting is always punished.'

(From: 101 SCHOOL ASSEMBLY STORIES: Carr)

2   Ask the pupils to comment on the story. You could lead with the following questions:

   a   Do you think Brer Rabbit was wicked or right in what he did? Was his trickery justified?

   b   Who do you think was the hero? Why?

   c   Does the biggest or strongest person always win in life? Can you give other examples?

   d   How effective was it to teach the lesson in this way? What will make you remember that 'pride comes before a fall'?

3   Now ask the pupils to see if they can write a fable to show people a truth in life.
     They can either make up a fable using their own characters and choosing their own ideas about what they want to teach people, or they may choose one of the following suggestions:

CHARACTERS	LESSON
A cat and a mouse	Brains are better than brawn
A cat and a goldfish	Never trust a flatterer
A butterfly and a moth	Beauty is in the eye of the beholder
A bee and a rabbit	Save for the future
The grass and the oak tree	It is easier to go with others than against them
Fire, air, water and earth	We all have a part to play in life

Miscellany

Classroom Quizzes

Quizzes are always useful to have on hand. They are entertaining as well as constructive ways of making pupils think about their language. The following examples could be used with classes, divided into teams or groups, offering correct answers to questions put by the teacher. (Dictionaries will be found helpful for most exercises.)

34 IDIOMS (Levels B & C)

In everyday speech we often use idioms wihout being aware of them and yet, when seen in written form, they can often seem ambiguous and misleading.

Explain the meaning of the following well-known idioms.

a   She made a waspish remark about him.

b   He hadn't seen them for donkey's years.

c   They chaired him off the field.

d   She left the job under a cloud.

e   He blamed the problems on red tape.

f   He was given the boot for throwing a spanner in the works.

g   They caught him red-handed.

h   He was feeling a little under the weather.

i   The news knocked him for six.

j   They couldn't see the wood for the trees.

k   She was very catty about his wife wearing the trousers.

l   He gave the talk off the cuff.

m   He was always going against the tide.

n   She was feeling extremely blue.

o   The black sheep of the family eventually found himself a plum job.

p   It's no good crying over spilt milk.

q   The problem was a thorny one.

r   She was very green when she started.

s   She had cold feet when she went for the interview.

t   He was told to stop talking through his hat.

u   He had them on the mat.

v   Everything was at sixes and sevens.

w   The manager was hand in glove with the directors.

x   She soon put a spoke in their wheel.

y   They were hoping to buttonhole the man in the corridor.

z   She was left out in the cold because she was wet.

35   FIFTY IMPOSSIBLE SPELLINGS!   (Levels B & C)

tortoise	dahlia
vaccinate	rhododendron
threshold	ecclesiastical

variegated

amnesia

misshapen

paraffin

pneumonia

millennium

magnanimous

posthumous

chlorophyll

dissension

hieroglyphics

infinitesimal

loathsome

illicit

questionnaire

anxiety

fuchsia

cyclamen

rebellion

vehemently

valedictory

forty

gnome

liquefy

battalion

chrysalis

guttural

intrigue

saccharine

sciatica

rhapsody

criticism

broccoli

labyrinth

pseudonym

parasol

isosceles

paraphernalia

philatelist

panicky

rhetorical

veterinary

rendezvous

pageant

36 SILENT LETTERS (Levels A, B & C)

There are a number of letters which form the spelling of words that are not actually sounded at all. This is one of the reasons why the

English language is so intriguing. Below are some examples. Ask the pupils to find as many as they can within a given time limit (say, 5 minutes).

silent B

Climb, crumb, debt, doubt, dumb, indebted, lamb, limb, numb, redoubt, subtle, thumb.

silent C

Abscess, abscind, indict, scene, scent, sceptre, science, scimitar, scissors, victuals.

silent CH

Schism.

silent G

Arraign, assign, campaign, consign, deign, design, ensign (which is accented on the first syllable), foreign, gnash, gnat, gnaw, gnome, gnostic, gnu, reign, resign, sign, sovereign.

silent GH

Blight, bright, bough, caught, delight, fight, flight, fright, height, high, light, might, naught, neighbour, nigh, night, ought, plight, plough, right, sigh, sight, slight, slough, straight, taught, thigh, tight, weight, wrought.

silent H

Heir, honest, honour, hour.

silent K

Knack, knapsack, knave, knead, knee, knew, knife, knight, knit, knob, knock, knoll, knot, knowledge, knuckle.

silent L

Balm, behalf, calf, calm, palm, psalm, salmon.

silent N

Autumn, column, condemn, hymn, solemn.

silent P

Corps, pneumatic, pneumonia, psalm, pseudo, psychic, pyschology, Ptolemy, receipt.

silent S

Island, isle, viscount.

silent UE

Catalogue, dialogue, epilogue, harangue, prologue, synagogue.

silent U

Colleague, guarantee, guard, guess, guest, plague, prologue, rogue, vague.

silent UGH

Although, bough, dough, nought, through.

silent W

Answer, sword, wrap, wreak, wreath, wreck, wren, wrench, wrestle, wretched, wriggle, wring, wrinkle, wrist, write, wrong.

37 FOREIGN PHRASES (Levels B & C)

We use many foreign phrases in our everyday lives. Do you know what the following mean?

faux pas	a mistake (social)
en masse	in a large number
à la carte	individually priced
à la mode	fashionable
ad lib	without planning
au fait	expert
bête noire	pet hate
bon voyage	a good journey
fait accompli	an accomplished fact
par excellence	of the highest order

carte blanche	freedom of action
coup d'état	violent over-throwing of the government
blasé	unappreciative
impasse	a position from which there is no escape
laissez-faire	lack of government interference
nom de plume	pen name
rapport	relationship
tour de force	feat of skill or strength
nota bene	note well **NB**
post mortem	after death/after the event
status quo	the unchanged original position
debacle	collapse, downfall, disaster
et cetera	and so on
gourmet	one who appreciates the best in food and drink
hoi polloi	the multitude
genre	type

38 PLURALS (Levels A, B & C)

English has different ways of showing the plurals of nouns. Can you provide the correct form of the plurals for the following. It is suggested that a correct answer earns a half mark, the other half mark being awarded if the whole word is correctly spelled.

eskimo	–s	innuendo	–(e)s
concerto	i	criterion	a
echo	–es	radio	–s
cupful	–sf—	ratio	–s

diagnosis	es	casino	−s
bureau	−x	motto	−es
studio	−s	crisis	es
terminus	i	datum	a
bacterium	a	banjo	−s
handful	−s	solo	−s
cameo	−s	ass	−es
tomato	−es	cargo	−es
passer-by	−s-by	erratum	a
oasis	es	formula	ae/−s
half	ves	court-martial	−s-martial
roof	−s	spoonful	−sf−
son-in-law	s-in-law	belief	−s

39 ABBREVIATIONS (Levels A, B & C)

We live in an age where abbreviations have become everyday usage, particularly in newspapers. What do the following abbreviations stand for?

NATO	North Atlantic Treaty Organisation
UNO	United Nations Organisation
UFO	unidentified flying object
Hi-Fi	high fidelity
FBI	Federal Bureau of Investigation
EEC	European Economic Community
AA	Automobile Association

RSVP	répondez s'il vous plait (reply, if you please)
LED	light emitting diode
TIR	Transports Internationaux Routiers (International Road Transport)
HP	hire-purchase (hp) horsepower
GMT	Greenwich Mean Time
HGV	heavy goods vehicle
LASER	light amplification by stimulated emission of radiation
UNESCO	United Nations Educational, Scientific and Cultural Organisation
USSR	Union of Soviet Socialist Republics
VAT	Value Added Tax
SAE	stamped, addressed envelope
ETA	estimated time of arrival
DJ	disc-jockey

vet	veterinary surgeon	fab	fabulous
bus	omnibus	super	superlative
flu	influenza	perm	permanent wave
lunch	luncheon	cab	cabriolet
plane	aeroplane	fan	fanatic
phone	telephone	pops	popular tunes
cinema	cinematograph	fridge	refrigerator
exam	examination	mike	microphone
pub	public house	trad	traditional
zoo	zoological gardens	mod	modern

Explain what is wrong with the following sentences or statements for 1 mark. Suggest a better, clearer way of giving the information for a second mark.

a   Wanted: a man to wash dishes and two waitresses.

b   Funerals: parking for clients only.

c   Cheap Sponge Roll: take a teacupful of flour and mix it with a teaspoon of caster sugar and a teaspoonful of baking powder; break two eggs into a cup, then slide into the mixture.

d   Emma found herself on a stool by the nursery fire. Securely pierced by a long brass toasting fork she held a piece of bread to the glowing flameless fire.

e   The old duke picked up a snapshot of a dear friend who had recently died on his bedroom mantlepiece.

f   Notice to milkman: Baby arrived yesterday. Please leave another one.

g   From a Parish magazine: All those wishing to give eggs to the needy are asked to lay them in the font.

h   Dining table for sale by lady with Queen Anne legs.

i   His mother only guessed the cause of his anxiety.

j   Notice in a laundrette: Please remove your clothes as soon as all the lights are out.

k   You won't catch a cold walking in the fresh air.

l   Nobody has been in the library for more than 10 minutes.

Record of Units Used

DATE	CLASS	UNIT	LEVEL	DATE	CLASS	UNIT	LEVEL

DATE	CLASS	UNIT	LEVEL	DATE	CLASS	UNIT	LEVEL